THE ARTISTIC CHILD

THE ARTISTIC CHILD

AVERY NIGHTINGALE

CONTENTS

1	Introduction	1
2	Understanding the Artistic Child	3
3	Encouraging Creativity at Home	5
4	Fostering Artistic Expression through Education	7
5	Developing an Artistic Mindset	9
6	Exploring Different Art Forms	11
7	Nurturing Innovation and Problem-Solving Skills	13
8	Supporting the Artistic Child's Emotional Well-bei	15
9	Building a Supportive Community for the Artistic C	17
10	Overcoming Challenges and Obstacles	19
11	Recognizing and Celebrating the Artistic Child's A	21
12	Conclusion	25

Copyright © 2024 by Avery Nightingale

All rights reserved. No part of this book may be reproduced in any manner whatsoever without written permission except in the case of brief quotations embodied in critical articles and reviews.

First Printing, 2024

CHAPTER 1

Introduction

Current educational and social systems have been designed to repress, or at best manage the expression of creativity in young children. Despite the fact that research yields substantial and continuous evidence of the importance for success and well-being to open the tap on abundant creativity in early school years, an artistic basis is intentionally withheld in the earliest years of formal education. Five human basic instincts include (but not limited to): perceptual, cognitive, artistic, communicative, emotional, and moral intuitions. In this piece, I would like to draw upon consideration of the further examination of the role of creativity as an innate biological mechanism that reflects the first five years in the life and the critical role played by the utilitarian fabric of a child's school in repressing the tap upon art.

For human beings, the creation of expressive art is wired into the brain by one and a half. From the first paintings and sculptures, compositional geometry can be seen in many examples of how young children call upon the collective visual experiences of humanity and current art events as they engage in producing their own individual images. In nearly half of the earliest drawings, young children's creations are observed to form iconic, schematic images that reflect the generic structure of a human figure or in experimental instances, a cat or a tree. Also, to reflect young children's intuitive understanding of kinetic actions, specific details, such as the fingers, toes, and neck are drawn as children gain increased command with their mark makers. Even objects drawn which are not human-like embody compositional features reflecting familiar shapes such as trees and flowers rounding the basis for the intuitive understanding of visual metaphors.

CHAPTER 2

Understanding the Artistic Child

When we introspect our lives, the argument we present in the following paragraphs becomes intuitive. We had a prime interest in music, art, mathematics, biology, and history, among other things, way before we received our first "real education." This exposes the generative spirit that naturally captivates children and bears their inherent uniqueness – and for that, Isaac Stern pronounces that "creative juices exist in all human beings and are, I believe, the very essence of life." It seems to us most natural that, as parents, dishwashers, bakers, and at kindred places, we exposed our preschool children to these faculties. Does it mean that we were perhaps not chained to rigid schedules, at all times physically present with our children, vigilant towards eating clover-free bread, wakeful about our family priorities, and the like? No, not at all. While there were times we were on a trip, but it was not through time and history; while there were times when work and various obligations delayed us, we were always there to pick up the pieces from a subsequent collision, be it with a bruising fourteenth-century suit of armor or a hyper-realistic wax figure which was supposed to have remained still at least for a quarter, or even a supermarket window.

In order to understand the artistic child, we need to be in tune with dynamics that foster a creative soul in the first place. This requires recognizing, understanding, and nurturing habits of mind often considered expendable in this day and time. Before anything else, we should recount our inherent thirst for creativity and the artful and imaginative dispositions we possessed at a tender age. It is only in doing so that we are better positioned to guide our children in exploring creative territories, much of which are not formally acknowledged in mainstream K-12 educational systems. As such, exploration and development of these critical and rich habits of mind and spirit in our young ones should be encouraged at home. Our school curriculums can enhance such exploration, but certainly not at the expense of systematic and unidimensional focus on all shades of standardized and high-stakes testing.

CHAPTER 3

Encouraging Creativity at Home

Recall a time when the people around you acted, momentarily, as artists. And then imagine growing up in a world – not the entire world perhaps, but our shared world, with our friends and our work and traffic and grumbles and lullabies – suffused with this attention. That word suffused is exactly what creativity needs because that is exactly what a young child is. They are possessed of a creativity potentially stilled by the Weltanschauung of all the world about, a belief that creativity properly comes only in the restricted circumstances of the artist's studio or the sterile freedom of a standardless mind. Just as the religious consciousness is one that feels at home in the presence of God, a talent-formed consciousness feels at home in the presence of talent.

Are we doing the most to cultivate our child's natural creative talents? Are we taking into account what neuroscientists have told us about the plasticity of the young child's brain and the conditions necessary for optimal creative growth? Do schools respect the research that shows that creative artists, scientists, and entrepreneurs are all alike in crucial respects? And what should we do when a young creative mind is constantly bored in school? Looking after a young child requires a lot of effort, and encouraging creativity may require even more. The term we should use in English for what a parent of young children needs to be is another familiar one from another time. We need to be an artist. Instead in modern English an artist is not someone living down the street who's doing something interesting, someone who says things that need to be said. Instead an artist is someone who is somehow special, and we might claim to be one ourselves; certainly our children have something to do with art.

CHAPTER 4

Fostering Artistic Expression through Education

What if we went back to this well-researched understanding and allowed these approaches to be used more broadly? What if we spent resources to understand our children more, employing this understanding to develop ways for tailoring their educational experience to encourage engagement and interest, motivating them to desire to continue to stretch and learn throughout their later years? The answer is clear – by nurturing the natural creativity of all children to create this type of environment, one ends up developing curious, educated, and motivated individuals. As a result, one would be read as a society to be more competitive on a global basis; capable of achieving outlandish breakthroughs and spawning broad innovative ventures that would touch everyone in the populace. Given the "spit-out" nature of our current educational system, individuals who graduate are forced to experience a conform culture or face severe financial constraints, further helping to eliminate what little internal motivation many students have for creating or learning new things.

The educational system in the United States was deliberately designed to concern itself with readying about 20% of its pupils for university, with very little concern for the other 80%. It was not until the late 1920s when the Committee on Problems of Education, which operated under the National Research Council, published its famous eight-year study, that the focus changed. The study's findings indicated that children benefited significantly from their time spent learning through practical, hands-on experiences focusing on solving problems rather than in ordinary "textbook style" teaching. Yet, while children under the age of 8 are able to approach learning in this natural and engaging manner, at about age 8, students start to "graduate" into a more traditional curriculum.

CHAPTER 5

Developing an Artistic Mindset

Attitude of the Artist. The attitude of the artist is confidence in one's heart and mind that quality effort will lead to a quality result. Thus, it is necessary to reassure the child that when met with failures, as in the words of an artist, "You adapt, you revise, you try something else, but then always with a sense of confidence on your shoulder." Nurturing an attitude of self-assurance must be in Clarisa's heart and in her mind that she is making a great effort, that it is worthwhile and that her sculpture is important. Like Clarisa, children participate in works of merit that require approval from parents, teachers, and other adults, and it is necessary for them to walk confidently and demand respect for their work. Parents, then, need to display confidence in the artist and reverence for the works of their children.

Teachers and parents can encourage students' focus on process and technique rather than the product, help them learn from mistakes and persevere in the face of failure, and keep open minds about unusual approaches. Nurturing an attitude of self-assurance in heart and mind and of determination to persevere with works of merit is the attitude underlying the innovative mind. Writers, artists, and other creative persons foster new ideas until they become works of merit, confronting and resolving numerous critiques, lack of money or materials, and doubts about the correctness of their approach, attitude, and effort.

CHAPTER 6

Exploring Different Art Forms

Being creative means knowing how to educate in the different forms of art and being aware, as Luigi Pirandello said, that for each form of genius understood as "thinking differently with respect to another standard genotype," it is necessarily also linked to a form of madness. The concept becomes even more evident in today's society, which considers different the one that does not fit into precise standards. The artist and the engineer must therefore both have that degree of madness that is however essential to create the new. It is no coincidence that our society is based on a dual division between science and art, between the humanistic and the scientific side. This separation, present since the time of Descartes, derives from a primordial point inserted within our thought. In fact, today it is still rooted in the minds of children: books, films, or programs continue to promote the image respectively the classic man from mythology and that of the absolute number or machine.

Painting is just one of many artistic forms with which a young mind might experiment. Every form of creation, whether technical or artistic, is a form of communication. I find a different way to tell the story of the world and of myself. Among the many forms of art, every child is likely to find the one that really allows him to express himself to the fullest of his potential. Good motor skills are a common code between all these forms of creativity. Like all muscles, they need to be trained. Children need to learn how to hold a pen or a brush. It is important, however, not to force the child's natural inclination. There are children who, for example, do not stand still in front of a paint roller, neither to stain the cheeks nor to move. Other children are able to use it as a means of expression and there is nothing to do if they are lucky enough to be able to do it without getting dirty and with someone else's roller. It is important for a child to work more easily if the work naturally tends to the creative side, rather than live in a time of forced expression, resulting in a predilection for the rational side. The body develops following one's genetic and natural inclinations. In other words, it is man who shapes matter, not the other way around.

CHAPTER 7

Nurturing Innovation and Problem-Solving Skills

Nurturing environmental factors (such as frequent exposure to a creative-rich environment and the non-critical observation of familiar models) are particularly strong predictors of later creativity, according to Rogers and Parry. Children who find avenues for creativity and problem-solving in classrooms, according to Flint and Snyder, depend on teachers who create a classroom environment allowing self-expression. Researchers at MIT learned from a decade-long study that to encourage children's problem-solving and invention skills, teachers may need to rethink the subject matter and goals of student academic content because of the way that children are naturally inclined to experimenting with what they know when placed in an interesting, problem-based setting. add that children are not creative in isolation and that social pressures may both encourage their behaviors (fostering a culture where creativity is respected and seen as contributive) and repress their behaviors (encouraging education that discourages social bonds and free-play).

Englander argues that education should be the home of creative instruction fostering originality and discovery, but points out that school, as the gatekeeper and arbiter of societal expectations, often fails to sustain children's natural inquisitiveness. The creative child sees what no one has yet seen, seizes that unseen thing, takes a risk and runs with an idea until just the right expression for that idea is captured, a process that often ends in discoveries yet to be made. This belief led to examine ways that technology may allow children to fulfill their potential and to suggest that the role that parents and other adults in a child's life play in defining creativity for the child, for the artists inside each child, is pivotal. In adults and teachers, children look for protection, exceptionality, intellectual curiosity and a model for overcoming barriers.

CHAPTER 8

Supporting the Artistic Child's Emotional Well-bei

Micenheimer suggests the following strategies to support the emotional well-being of gifted students in any domain of talent, including visual and constructing arts:
1. Limit expectations to what the student is capable of at the present time by not overtasking him with creating something beyond his ability. 2. Constantly demonstrate support for the giftedness of the student's work to ensure that he is comfortable considering himself a talented individual. 3. Foster the growth of leadership by allowing the student to mentor and help guide others. As a mentor, the student can share his talent by providing options to others beyond his level of creativity as an artist. 4. Test the child's ability as a leader by allowing him to pick out a project that he may lead other students in executing. 5. Collaboration provides social interaction and gives the artist and other students opportunities to explore new ideas and techniques to add to their repertoires as artists.

Another way to promote the development of the whole gifted child is through the aspects of emotional learning activities that support artistic identity. Artistic identity is important because it can foster in a child the confidence and support that the student needs to pursue his talents. Belenky and Atkins use the terms "Voice" and "Silencing the Voice". "Voice" is a precursor of deeper learning about artistic identity. The opposite is "Silencing the Voice" which causes individuals to give in to the negative stereotypes and shut down their creative or artistic talents. Silent Voices have not yet realized that their ideas, thoughts, and personal perspectives are just as important and necessary to collaborative visionary work as the ideas of those around them. Once "Voice" has been established, the next step is to introduce the developing artist to "Knowledge of Self" using concepts based on Howard Gardner's seven intelligences.

CHAPTER 9

Building a Supportive Community for the Artistic C

- Put together a "creative corner". This is a space within your home where all creative materials are housed. This way, everything is right there when you want to do art. This creative corner should be where your child can have free range to access any materials at any time. They should always know where their art materials are and feel comfortable getting them out. This shows them that you value their art and believe in their abilities. Children who have access to lots of materials, whether they know how to use them all or not, have an increased ability to develop creatively.

The following is a list of suggestions for the parent of an artistic child:

One great way to encourage the creative process in art is to help create an environment conducive to creativity. This can be done at home and/or at school, and is generally broken down into the following components: providing a time and place for the artistic child to be creative, guilt-free time, understanding the creative process, inspiration, and necessary materials. You, as the parent, have the most influence on the early creative experiences of the artistic child. How do you develop a home environment that nurtures creativity and innovation?

CHAPTER 10

Overcoming Challenges and Obstacles

Generation after generation, educators have been responsible for upholding prescribed systems in order to maintain the masses. We have kept our thought leaders, musicians, inventors, and revolutionaries tethered and labeled. We have imposed gender limitations, mostly unaware that collectively they have left an indelible impact on how differences are upheld, viewed, and/or destroyed. A civilization cannot remain as it was fifty years ago. Simplification is the key if we're stuck. Simplifying until complex can be mastered. Simplifying is easily achieved by asking for critical thinking from our children. Simplifying is asking for opinions and allowing oneself to be flexible when nothing is as seen or portrayed. Offer children the luxury for stewardship over topics to be elaborated, practiced, and completed without being told: What are we fixing now? Where is your source? This book is not in our list - can I see this book before you use it?

As a parent, you already know and understand the complexities of learning to ride a bike, potty training, and crawling through life's beloved obstacles. You understand life is filled with challenges and obstacles. To stand in the way of meeting challenges and overcoming them is detrimental to raising an artistic child. The Literacy Garden is no different than life's loved physical surroundings. Encourage in children the ability to surpass expectations and master the challenges that inspire them. Inspired literacy gardens are responsible for contributing to a civilization and must be maintained to assure rich, complex learning environments. They are places of trust, respect, and inspiration that value the imagination. Until we can overhaul the national marathon of student standardization, as parents and educators, we must maintain gardens that rise above mediocrity and blossom pathways for others to travel.

CHAPTER 11

Recognizing and Celebrating the Artistic Child's A

One emotion should not be driven by a single point of reference. Each author will provide a distinct and unique vision; boys and girls us a story, a personal story obtained from the dispute and relation with the situations of their life, among which they include school and surrounding society. No child systematically eulogizes parents or professors. But it disserves us to accuse them of lying should they opt to describe their family or school with expressions opposite to the supposed truth. To best understand the infinite variety of affective situations present in a society is to transform the plural dynamics of education and art. In the contrast between the conceptions expressed by children and our artistic experience as adults with more elaborate conceptual parameters, we who are committed to pedagogy become increasingly mindful to the limitations of our prosumer posturing, as though it were in the hands of the adult to know by himself/herself and instruct with mastery the content and the objectives that continuously pass through the educative relations between people. Art and pedagogy expose to us the rich differences between children and adults. Important, necessary, and relevant education is the potential to let itself share by childish values and criteria, with their experiences and feelings.

Our conversations with students lead us toward another characteristic of defined challenges: namely, the role of personal achievement in artistic experience. When asked why art was so important to them, students told us (as did parents and teachers) that through art they can make their thoughts, feelings, and identity visible. With their art, they say, "I tell my story"; "I can really see what I think about something"; "I can put myself into the world"; "I show myself in a way no one can understand when I speak or write"; "I can be known." When we look at children's drawings, we often seem embarrassed when we find that these young people have ideas and perceptions of tremendous depth. This can happen so frequently that we might be inclined to suppose that the adults involved with these children are mere victims of their emotions, letting the children do as they please and still aware at some level that they themselves are the true sources of ideas and actions. In other responses, adult audiences may discover children to be devoid of reality because, they conclude, bestiality is what characterizes all works produced by little ones. Therein lies the complicated relation we, as adults, have with art, with children, and with their art. We recognize art as a fertile space for the development of people and for the construction of human culture; however, we relegate it to infancy, intuition, memory, or to the self-expression of simple little ones. Our suppositions and also our experiences erroneously take us away from the creative and humanizing richness of children's art. We may not realize it. But the consequences of such a stance shape the society that surrounds these children. Teachers who teach above all with the goal of obtaining an aesthetic production from children and families favor forms of control, coercion, and incentive that perpetuate the caricature of art instruction inside the schools today. Reinforcing such a perspective, despite our good intentions and verified reasoning, we belittle and humiliate thousands of little people who are unjustly suffering even in the light of their own educative processes.

CHAPTER 12

Conclusion

On the natural selection and survival level, we are far from being the fastest, the strongest, the largest, or the most plentiful in number, yet we continue growing in numbers and in capabilities. Greater articulation, dexterity, ambidexterity, questioning, and diversity in thinking are strong examples that have grown in humans over the years, and they will continue. As teachers, from early childhood through graduate education, how do we treat those features? Are they treated as distinct and unrelated as separate pieces, or are they treated as breathlessly overlapping elements corresponding beautifully time after time and fact after fact? Synergy is seen in so many examples in history. Man has seen fit to record his genius so that all can learn from it and grow with it. Such individuals have been artists as well as scientists, inventors as well as mathematicians. The artistic child is the thriving child. The artistic adult is the productive, creative thriving adult.

In this book, we have stressed the importance of artistic and creative development for the optimization of a child's full learning potential. As our world changes, we find that we are becoming more and more interested in those capabilities that all of us humans have in common – our creativity and imagination. Mathematician, scientist, and philosopher Alfred North Whitehead wrote: "It is a profoundly erroneous truism, repeated by all copybooks and by eminent people when they are making speeches, that we should cultivate the habit of thinking of what we are doing. The precise opposite is the case." The opposite or "complementary habit" as he refers to it is that we become "capable of playing with the whole universe of our experiences and the resultant general ideas with the same sort of attraction with which a child plays with its games." This is not just about art, this is about all aspects of creativity and imagination and therefore, "The principle of joy as the source of creative artistic activity becomes one of the conclusions of the development." What do we want for our children and for ourselves as adults? What does our society need in the future? Are we nurturing that which is absolutely unique to the human experience and that which sets us distinctly apart from all other living things?

Milton Keynes UK
Ingram Content Group UK Ltd.
UKHW031352011224
451755UK00004B/368